The School of Get Shit Done:

*How Imperfect Action Leads to
Success In Life and Business*

This book is dedicated to my wife and kids.

Thank you for always believing in me and pushing me to be my very best.

Table of Contents

Foreword

When it comes to getting shit done, I know Chad to handle business like no other. As a matter of fact, I've personally worked with Chad over the last 15 months and I can tell you he has 10X'd everyone else I've got. While most people in my Tribe have 1-5 funnels, Chad has over 80. The dude literally gets shit done.

I'm a well-known action taker myself, and it takes one to know one. The fact that Chad wrote and published this book in less than a month, gives him the credibility to talk about taking massive action. Chad is one of the most prolific action takers I've ever met. There are a lot of lessons to be learned from a man with this many experiences.

You don't gain expertise without experiments and without being an action taker, you don't experiment. Chad is a true expert and the outline of how he got to where is, lies within the covers of this easy to read, fast paced, book of stories of success and failure.

This book leaves you hanging on every chapter. It reads more like a short novel than some boring business book. You'll find yourself struggling to put the book down after the first couple of chapters. You'll feel like you need to see the story all the way to the end.

Here's the thing though. I know Chad well enough to say this on his behalf. He didn't write this book for you just to sit there, read it, and feel good about his progress. He wrote it so you'd get up, get out, and get shit done!

Ryan Stewman

Hardcore Closer

Introduction

In this book, I'm going to share with you the many successes and failures that helped shape my life into what it is today. I'm going to discuss my rise in corporate America, which came about by doing what I was supposed to do, making a six-figure living, and living comfortably. I'm also going to tell you about my fall. How I became broke, with no idea how I was going to pay our bills or provide for my family. When I was going through these challenges I felt the hopelessness and doubt. I wondered if I would ever get out of this place of fear and vulnerability.

I had to fail and hit a very low and dark place in my life before I realized a few things. 1.) I wasn't going to be successful until I started betting on myself; and 2.) No one is going to come save you! The only person who can control your life and make the changes you want to make is you

I share my lessons to inspire you. I am no different from the millions of people out there, except I would not allow myself to be defeated. Quitting and failure have never been, nor will they ever be, an option for me.

I want you to see that if you put in the time, effort, and work, then you can be successful in life and business. The power of imperfect action will accelerate you into a whole new stratosphere. Life is hard and will only get harder. Your success is solely dependent upon you. I hope you will enjoy reading this book as much as I've enjoyed writing it. This has been a soul-searching experience. I had to be honest with myself about what I did well; where I went wrong; and how I got to where I am today.

I learned the art of "Imperfect Action" Imperfect action is getting up every day and working towards your goals. You may not have it all figured out, but you do know the direction you want to go and what needs to be done. This is how to implement imperfect action into your business to stand out.

I hope my story inspires you.

Chapter 1

The Lie -
My Parents, Teachers, and
Society

When I was a kid my parents fucking lied to me. Before you say, "Well, that really sucks for you," don't worry, your parents lied to you, too.

You may ask yourself, "What is this great lie?" The lie is that if you go to school and get good grades, you'll get a good job, live a nice life, and have a nice little retirement. This couldn't be further from the truth.

We are taught by society that living safe, living paycheck to paycheck, is how it should be done. We are taught the "right way" is to follow in our parents' footsteps. That means you go to school and get good grades. Then you'll find a good job and work for 30 years. After that, you're going to get a nice retirement and live on that until the day you die. What they don't tell you is that your retirement is a fraction of what you made as income before retirement, and that retirement eventually runs out.

Very few people ever save up enough money to retire and live the lifestyle they lived when they were working. It takes approximately 1 million dollars in a retirement fund to yield an annual payout of approximately $40,000 per year. If you are only making $40,000 per year, then it is going to take an extremely long time to save up $1,000,000 dollars. If you are making over $100,000 per year, it may be easier to save up $1,000,000, but you are never going to be able to live off of the $40,000 in retirement per year. It is a vicious cycle that seems to plague many people as they grow older and retire.

Things are different now than they were back when our parents' parents were growing up. I see people getting 30 year mortgages at 50 and 60 years old. Most of those people will never pay-off a house. How could they? They have been living paycheck to paycheck for so many years that there is not enough money to take a family vacation, let alone pay extra toward a home. The lie our parents told us was meant to institutionalize us and make us think that everything is going to be OK.

Twenty years later, we now have an entire generation of entitled brats who don't want to work hard. They're inherently lazy. They don't come into the job force and say, "What can I do to help your company grow?" They come into the job force and say, "Well, what kind of changes are you going to make to suit me, because I'm a millennial?" As parents, we are failing our children by not making them work for anything. We give them everything they could ever want on a silver platter and then wonder why they look at us like we owe them something! Participation trophies and the idea that everyone is a winner is hurting our country, not helping it.

I hear it from teachers and parents all the time. "We don't want to stress our children out." "We don't want to tell them that they are not number 1." "We don't need to keep score and lower their self-esteem when they do not win."

Last time I checked the world was keeping score. Not everyone gets a trophy. Some people make more money than other people. They live in bigger homes and drive fancier cars. When do we want our kids to learn this lesson? When they are adults and they look back and are now resentful because the world is not full of rainbows and kittens?

I am just as guilty as the next guy at spoiling my kids rotten. My 14-year old and 8-year old each have a 50-inch plasma TV hanging on their bedroom walls. Neither one of them need a television that big. My son doesn't need a television that big to play XBOX. The difference is I explain to them that they have those things because their mother and father work very hard for them and they need to appreciate them as they can be taken away very quickly.

I lived the lie for many years. When I was younger I believed it too. Why not? My parents said it was true so I should believe it. But then something very scary happened to me. I went to school and got good grades. I did everything that society said was the normal route to take to be successful. I graduated in the top 10 percent of my high school class. I graduated in the top of my college class, with a degree in international business, and I couldn't find a job. What the hell?

I'm writing this book to inspire other salespeople, entrepreneurs, and any other people who are looking for a different path to success. It wasn't until I realized that the old way, the way society teaches, is only making someone else rich. Don't get me wrong. The rich love this system. It is a game and they are the only ones who know the rules.

Chapter 2

Parents' Story

My parents didn't mean to lie to me. If anything, they had the best intentions and they loved me. I was their only child. Just like any parent, they wanted to see me become successful. The problem was that my parents' view of success was very different from what fuels and drives entrepreneurs and successful business people.

Their view of success was to play it safe and follow what society tells you is normal.

As I said before, they stressed going to school, getting good grades and getting into a good college so that after graduation I would find a nice, steady job, working for somebody and making them rich. Then I'd get a nice retirement. That type of mentality may have worked 30, 40, and 50 years ago but it doesn't work in 2016.

When I got out of college, I couldn't find a job to save my life. With a college degree in International Business I could not find a job! I ended up taking a job that I was completely ashamed to tell people about. I'm sure my parents thought, "What did we just pay for?" It was not that I was not willing to work hard. I just had no direction as I chose a very different career path from what my parents deemed as normal. More on that later.

My parents were teachers, both highly educated, and worked in the same line of work for more than 30 years. They lived a very conservative lifestyle. We lived in a nice home in a nice middle class community. My parents didn't overspend, because there wasn't a whole lot of extra money on a teacher's salary. I was not the kid that got Jordan's just because I wanted them. My parents had no problem telling me that there was not extra money for silly things like $100 shoes.

They were taught that if you go to work, you will get a nice, steady paycheck every two weeks so you know your income is going to be the same and steady. From there, you just budget to live each month on less than you make, and everything should be fine. The problem was that often there was more "month" than income. The other problem with was my parents were committed to their careers, but no matter how hard they worked or how many hours they put in their paycheck did not change. That is what too many people face today.

I want to be very clear that I was not raised poor. We were middle-class, very middle of the row. My parents had a steady income. We had a beautiful home. It wasn't large, but it was enough for us. I did not feel at the time the home was too small. It is only when I look back on what the media and society say the "right" size home should be, that I feel that it was small. I was the only child. I never really did without, but, as I got older, I noticed that my parents sacrificed a lot for me to have a little. My parents put my needs before their own. I love them very much for it. That is what parents are supposed to do. You love your kids and you want them to have all the things you didn't growing up. Their sacrifices helped me become successful in many areas.

I want to do things differently for my kids. I want to help them understand the value of the dollar and that you only get to have the things you want if you work hard and bring value to the marketplace. The marketplace will determine how much you get paid by whether or not clients and employers are willing to pay you for your services. So many times people believe they are more valuable than they really are. We have an entire generation of people that believe when they get out of school they should become the boss and make the big check without ever stepping foot in the workforce. I want to teach them that there is a different way than just going through the day mindlessly working for someone else. Not having that thrill of building something for your family isn't necessarily the right way to do it.

I want to teach them that there is a different way than just going through the day mindlessly working for someone else. Not having that thrill of building something for your family isn't necessarily the right way to do it. I'm not knocking the 8-5 job with the same steady pay every two weeks. But, if that's your mentality, then this book probably isn't for you.

The type of mentality that I have is that you have the ability to accomplish anything that you want to accomplish, no matter where you come from or what you've been taught. I believe that if you are going to work hard you should make as much money as you possibly can because it can be taken away from you very quickly. You have to protect what you earn because every day there is someone out there working twice as hard to take what you have.

I hope that I am teaching my children a different way to think. I hope I'm giving them an opportunity to fail while it's safe. I want them to try new things while I can still bail them out. I don't want their first attempts at greatness or their first failure to be in an environment in which I cannot help them and guide them. I want to use each failure as a teachable moment to make sure they learn something valuable from it. Each opportunity to learn is an opportunity to get better.

One of the things my parents taught me was an extremely good work ethic. What they didn't necessarily teach me was the best way to go about becoming wealthy. Wealth doesn't mean you are going to be happy, but I know one thing for sure. I have been broke. I am way happier bringing value to the market place, helping people achieve financial success and having money in my bank account than I ever was when I could not afford to buy food.

I can remember a time when my parents told me that if I wanted to become a teacher, that they would not pay for college. I actually looked at them kind of funny, thinking, "Well, why not be a teacher? We've lived a very comfortable life. Being a teacher isn't bad. We've got a nice home. We don't do without."

But my parents saw so much more in me. They actually sat me down and said, "Chad, you can be anything that you want to be. We didn't work so hard and constantly push you so you could just be a teacher. You can be an engineer. You can be a doctor. You can be a lawyer. Don't settle for something that you don't love."

My parents loved their jobs. But I learned something from watching them for 30 plus years, going to the same job day after day. No matter how much they worked, how much extra time they put in, or how much they sacrificed for their careers, their paycheck never became bigger. Their paycheck was always the same.

Some people are OK with that, and that's fine. But everyone has one life to live. It's totally up to you what you do with it. You have the ability for greatness, so don't limit yourself based on what society says you should do.

Our Society teaches us that we deserve to have shit. I work, I want it, so therefore I should have it. We have become a society of instant gratification. If you disagree, then tell me how you feel the next time you text your friend or email someone at work and they wait until the next day to respond. This idea that if I want it, I should have it is one of the many reasons we have an entire generation of kids that feels entitled. It's another reason that credit card debt is astronomical.

I hope that my parents are proud of me when they look down from Heaven at what I've accomplished. Losing them was one of the hardest things I have had to overcome in my life. It is not easy and there are days it is still down right unbearable. I learned so much from them by the way they loved life and believed in family.

Chapter 3

The Girl

Every good story needs a love story. My love story started in 1992 when I met Hope, the girl of my dreams. I took a different approach in everything in my life; some good, some bad.   If you have met the person who is destined to be your soul mate then you know how intense that feeling is. The problem with me and many guys is that when a guy likes a girl they revert back to kindergarten when they said mean things and pulled her hair.

I've been able to accomplish many things through hard work, dedication, and desire, including getting the girl. But as you will see here I was not as good of a sales person as I am today. I was not closing any deals in her mind and I am damn lucky she didn't walk out of my life early on.

The first time Hope and I met, it didn't go over so well. I was actually hanging out with some friends one night and she was there. She was excited because she was there to show one of my friends, actually her boyfriend at the time, a dress for their prom. Needless to say, I was a snot-nosed little kid, full of confidence. When she popped out of the car and showed this dress to my friend, the first thing I said was, "Oh, isn't that special?"

Now, what I really was thinking was, "Man, I bet she's going to look great in that dress." But my ego and little smart mouth couldn't say that. I couldn't let my friend know that I was eyeing his girlfriend. That wouldn't be the right thing to do. So, I reverted back to what I learned in kindergarten: if you like a girl, you pull her hair, you pinch her and just act plain mean toward her. I knew immediately that she was the one.

As you can imagine she did not take too kindly to me shitting on her big moment. Here she was a senior and I was just a lowly underclassman. Even as a sophomore, I knew I had skills, but I had not yet honed them in. I had no problem talking to most girls and dated quite a few, including most of the older cheerleaders at our school.

This endeavor was not going as planned. I had reverted back to a tactic that had not worked well in kindergarten either and she made it very well known she was not impressed. I tried to play it off like it did not bother me, but I really felt bad for the way I had acted. Unfortunately, my ego would not let me apologize.

A few years went by and I ran into Hope again. This time things were a little bit different. I had a girlfriend and she had a boyfriend, but I didn't let my mouth or my attitude get in the way. My girlfriend at the time was actually the manager at a store in the mall and a couple of my friends worked there. Hope decided that she wanted to work there because it was a cool place where all the high school kids would come and hang out. You basically got to hang out with your friends but get paid. This was in the early 90's, so working at a pager and phone store in the mall would have been a dream job for any kid right out high school.

My buddy, Wayne, was working there and he and Hope knew each other from high school. They had some mutual friends so it was not that hard for her to get the job. Once she got the job, I started seeing her on a regular basis. We were friendly to each other, but nothing was going to happen. I knew she had a boyfriend and I had been in a relationship at this time with her manager. Remember how I said I had closing skills at a young age? I was 17 at the time and my girlfriend was 21. It didn't suck to have a girlfriend who could buy alcohol. At the same time, there was obviously some attraction between Hope and me. I would make it a point to flirt with her when my girlfriend wasn't around. There was a lot of playful bantering going back and forth but we both knew nothing was going to come of it.

Then one day it happened. My girlfriend had left the country for a vacation and when she got back it was very apparent that things were not the same. We did not see each other as often and our communication levels had broken down. While she was in another country on vacation she decided she wanted to cheat on me and thought things would go back to normal when she got back. I was really hurt, but looking back, I was already starting to develop feelings for Hope. I just hadn't let her know. When my girlfriend and I broke up, I asked Hope if she'd be willing to go out with me.

What do you think she said? That's right, she said, "Nope." She remembered how I had treated her a year and a half earlier, making fun of her pretty dress. She was going to show me. Like with anything else, I was pretty stubborn. At this point, I knew I was a salesperson, so the word *no* didn't mean a whole lot to me. I devised a plan to be able to take her out on a date. I had to figure out a way to not only impress her, but to show her that I wasn't the complete jerk she remembered from a couple of years ago.

One night I got this great idea (not); I put a rose under the windshield wiper of her car, so she would find it when she came

out after work. I even left a little note,
thinking that was going to seal the deal. She
tossed it in the trash and acted like it was
nothing. I have to admit. This was quite
the blow to my ego. I was used to getting
the girls I wanted to go out with to go out
with me. Like a said I don't take *no* for an
answer very well. I was persistent, and
after a few months of trying to court her,
she finally agreed to go out with me.

We went to a little local Chinese
restaurant down the road from the mall.
I'm not sure if that was because she didn't
want to be seen with me or because she
was looking for some alone time. I did not
care what the reason was. I just wanted to
get to know her and now was my
opportunity. In life, like in business, you
have to recognize the opportunities that are

in front of you or you will never close the deals.

What's really funny is that we've been together for 23 years now, and she doesn't even like Chinese food anymore. But we went to this little Chinese restaurant and had a great time. From that very first evening, I realized she and I were different. She was unlike anyone I'd ever been around. The way her family brought her up was completely different from the way my family raised me.

My parents were very conservative teachers. She came from a family of entrepreneurs. Her father owned a construction company. They knew what it meant to be in feast or famine. Her family moved here from Florida when she was very young because there was no work in

Florida. She remembered when her dad
would have to work outside of the state
because he had to follow where the work
went. Her brothers followed in the same
footsteps; one was in construction, one in
moving. All three of them were willing to
work hard and the more they worked, the
more they made.

She knew what it was like to be
without. She was very leery of my cocky,
arrogant ass. Remember, I wasn't rich, but I
definitely didn't do without. She taught me
a different mentality, that what you put into
something is what you get out of it. Hope
saw in me what I often did not see in
myself. She saw that I had the ability to
take massive action and put I the work
needed to be successful. She helped me
learn that I should have confidence in my

abilities.   Mainly, what she did for me, more than anyone since my parents, was support me unconditionally.

She supported the fact that school was important to me. I grew up playing tennis and became a nationally-ranked tennis player. I went to college on a scholarship. There will be a little bit more about that later. On the priority list of school, tennis and girlfriend, well, she was number three on that list. I had to go to school and I had to play tennis to have my scholarship. But she still supported me in everything I wanted to do.

Throughout this book you're going to see examples of where I received support from her, even in my biggest failures. Her ability to push me and challenge me to take imperfect action is what led me, and our family, to where we are today. She is now the mother of our two children and my best friend. I believe my life would be very different had we not met. I would not be where I am today as a person or an entrepreneur without her. She will never truly know how much I love her and appreciate her. She had many reasons over the years to give up on me, but stood right there beside me and helped me move forward every single time. She believed in me more than I ever believed in myself. Remember, I was taught to play it safe and she was taught to let it fly and chase your dreams.

Remember this as you're building your core. The relationships you maintain will have a direct reflection on whether you achieve success or end up with you sitting

on the sidelines and watching others
succeed.

Chapter 4

College Gameday

Going to college on a tennis scholarship was one of my proudest accomplishments. I worked hard while other friends were out partying and having a good time in high school. I was able to become state and nationally ranked, and I was able to help my parents pay for college. More than anything, college athletics taught me who I really was. It taught me how to control my competitiveness and use it to my advantage. But the story I'm about to tell you shows how that came completely crashing down.

In 1994, I was ranked in the top 20 tennis players in Texas. In my senior year of high school, my partner and I went to the state tournament in doubles. I was fortunate enough to get offered a scholarship to the number one junior college tennis team in the country, a school that had won several national titles. I could not have been more excited for the opportunity to go play there. I knew some of the guys from around Texas that I grew up competing against would be there.

I'd had success in both high school tennis and state tournaments, and now had an opportunity to go to the number one junior college team in the country. Needless to say, my ego was a little big. I can remember thinking that I was going to be the next big man on campus. I thought I was going to go there and dominate, continuing the same success that I had achieved up until that point. It was also going to be the first time that I moved away from home. I was going to learn to be my own man. It was the first time I had to do my own laundry, cooking, and everything on a consistent basis. But I was ready, because I had taken all the steps up until that point to be successful. I had been successful, and I was now being rewarded for my hard work.

So I went to Tyler Junior College, thinking that I was going to be the next big man on campus. When I got there, I found that because it is the number one team in the country, everyone who received offers to play at that school was a great player. There were people that flew in from all over the world. There were students that weren't on scholarship, who just flew in to try out and to walk on. People flew in from places like Peru, England, New Zealand, and Australia. Here I was, just a kid from Texas, thinking that my shit didn't stink and that they should be happy to have me. I was in for a whole new world. I did love the relationships that I built with the players from all over the world. Only, I wasn't the big man on campus. I was struggling to even find a spot.

I don't mind telling you, after being successful in so many things up until this point in my life, I didn't like it. My parents made me believe that if I just worked hard, it was my God-given right to be successful.

Being the egotistical maniac that I was, it was a slap in the face when I didn't get to play all the time. In college, there were no easy matches. Everyone is good at that level. The margin between winning and losing was not about who had better strokes, but who could handle the pressure with the most confidence. It wasn't like when I was in junior high or high school, where there would be a couple of easy matches and then from there, it got tougher and tougher as the tournaments moved along. Here, just the practices alone were challenging. I often found myself on the outside looking in, because there were only so many spots on the team. Up until that point, I had used my God-given athleticism to beat many players. Now I was in this place where I was no longer the best player. I wasn't even necessarily one of the top best players. I found myself fighting for a spot. My own ego and frustration made me not willing to put in the work at this new level. As a result, I often I found myself not getting an opportunity to play.

I decided that I was going to voice my concerns to the coach. Mind you, this is the number one team in the country. They didn't need me. The entire roster on that team was full of great players that were going to go on to play Division One on scholarships. I told the coach that I wasn't getting the playing time that I felt like I deserved. I had been taught that if you work hard, you deserve to play. If you work hard, you're going to be successful. I thought I was working hard, but when I honestly look back, I wasn't really working that hard. I was resting on my laurels. I felt like it was owed to me, and I had the same sense of entitlement that a lot of other people have today.

I voiced my concern. I pouted like a baby. I kicked and screamed. When nationals came around, I didn't get invited to go with the team. Because I was so stubborn, instead of going down there and supporting my team, I stayed at home with my parents and told the coach that I didn't want to come back the following year.

After I did that, and I got a chance to think about things, I realized that I was in the wrong, I tried to reach out to the coach. I tried to reach out to the players and let them know I had changed my mind. I wanted to come back. But the coach never returned my phone calls. After I'd told him that I was no longer interested, my spot was filled. My scholarship was taken.

Here I was, 19 years old, from one of the top teams in the country, and I have nowhere to go to school the following year because my big mouth and ego got me in trouble. How many times does this happen in sales? How often have we let our mouths talk us right out of the deal?

I learned from that experience that it doesn't matter what God-given talents you have if you're not willing to put in the work. If you're not willing to work harder than your competitor and harder than the guy standing next to you, you don't deserve shit. I also learned at a very young age that I was replaceable. I realized that I was just a number. In college athletics, you're there to make the university look good. In exchange, you get a free education. There were people there with not as much natural athletic ability as me, but they were willing to play and train much harder. They were willing to put forth the effort that I never was, because I wanted to hang out with my friends, have a good time, and enjoy the college experience. Those kids that were willing to work harder than me were rewarded. While I was willing to work to a certain degree, I also felt like it was owed to me.

Now, with no place to go, I transferred to The University of North Texas, a Division One school, that some friends attended. I was fortunate enough to receive a scholarship and I promised myself that I was going to put in the effort, work my ass off, and be the best that I could be this time.

Just like with everything else, Hope got behind me, and she said, "You can be anything that you want to be. If you want to be a top tennis player, you can do that." She transferred to the university I attended. I had one of the greatest years in my college career, because we both went to the same school. She was out there supporting me every weekend or every week during matches, as we played all over the country. She would even travel up to places like Oklahoma to watch matches.

Then, another setback came. The University of North Texas tennis team I was on cut their men's tennis team, due to Title Nine. Title Nine was implemented so that men and women had an equal number of scholarships. In theory, this was a good thing, but universities had to cut teams in order to be compliant. My team happened to be on the chopping block. I had worked so hard. I was playing in the top three or four at this university and was winning matches. I was called in one day, and they said, "We're not going to have a tennis team next year, and unfortunately, we are unable to renew your scholarship." Now I'm being kicked down after I think that I've done everything I need to do to be successful.

Fortunately, I had put my ego aside and put in the effort, and I had caught the attention of another school, The University of Texas at Arlington, about an hour south of Denton. The University of Texas at Arlington was actually a top 50 nationally ranked Division One school and they were interested in me. I went down there, and I met some of the greatest people that I'm still friends with today. I was given an opportunity to learn under a mentor who believed in me. He gave me an opportunity, and in reality, taught me what it meant to be an athlete and a man. I transferred there my junior year, and I was willing to put in the work. We were traveling all over the country for tournaments.

I was the happiest I've ever been, because I'd found a group of people that were like-minded individuals. They all wanted to work hard. They wanted to play hard. They held each other accountable. We went on to be nationally ranked, then went on to win multiple Southland Conference championships. Being part of a winning team is an amazing experience and learning tool.

I was able to bury my father with one of the rings that we won. That was a great honor for me. It was a way for me to pay him back, but more on that later. While I was at school there, I had to decide what I wanted to do for the rest of my life, because I realized I was not going to make it as a professional tennis player. I was good, but I wasn't good enough to earn a living. I knew that I didn't want to teach tennis at a country club. There's nothing wrong with that, but I didn't want to stand out in the 110-degree Texas heat, teaching bratty kids and old ladies how to play tennis. I had to figure out what I wanted to do with my life and which direction I was going to go.

That's when I decided to get a degree in International Business. At that time, NAFTA kicked in, and I thought, "Oh, man.

The North American Free Trade Agreement is going to give me the opportunity. I'm going to learn Spanish and I'm going to basically be rich. I'm going to travel all around the world."

At that time, Hope was still just my girlfriend, but I knew that she was the one. We would have been married sooner but both our parents adopted the idea that if we wanted to act like adults then they would treat us like adults. What that meant in a nut shell was there would be no more financial help in college if we were married. I knew she was the one and we would be married someday, so I went with the flow.

I had this idea though that we were going to travel all around. We were going to be rich. This is what society had told me. I remember sitting in business school hearing all of these wonderful theories of how life and business worked but had no idea if they would hold true in the real world.

I was in for a rude awakening as I found out later that the shit you read in books holds no weight in the real world. Life is a lot different when you're under fire to hit a deadline.

I was ready for the next chapter in my life. I graduated cum laude of the business school in 1999. I had this fantastic degree. I graduated with a high GPA. I looked like a real bad ass on paper, and I was ready to take the world by storm. Remember, my parents taught me if you go to school and you get good grades, you're going to get a good job. Here I was, 23 years old, graduating with a degree in International

Business, and I had no idea what I was going to do with my life.

Chapter 5

Now What?

Holy Fuck! I graduated. What was I going to do with my life? I had a college degree, and I couldn't find a job. I started to question all of the decisions I'd made up to this point. Hope stuck by me through school and tennis. Now we were graduated and she fully expected for us to get married. I couldn't find a fucking job. What was I going to do?

When you're desperate, you don't make the best decisions. That's why they always say it's easier to find a job when you have a job. Don't ever quit your job and start looking for another job. What did I do? I took the worst job I could have ever taken. I started answering ads in a local circular, *The Greensheet*, and in the newspaper. Remember, this was before Jobs.com, Monster.com, LinkedIn or any of these other career sites. I saw this job listing, and it read, "Advancement opportunity, sales." So I took the job. When I say this was the worst job, I mean it. Let me explain.

I was the guy who was out on the college campuses getting people to fill out credit card applications for t-shirts, koozies, and pens. That's right, I spent four and a half years getting a degree in International

Business, and now I'm on college campuses getting kids to fill out credit card applications so I can make $1.25 per application. Boy, were my parents proud of me.

Hope and I were now married. She told me that I could be anything I wanted to be and supported me in everything I did. How in the world would she get behind me and this shitty career choice? It had me questioning all of my choices. I had graduated top of my class, and was told that I was going to be successful. I couldn't get hired. This is the only job I could find. Where did I go wrong?

Now, Hope is a smart woman. Remember, she had a different mindset than me. Her mindset was that you don't go work for someone else and make them rich.

After two days, I think I had made a
whopping $12 because I was too fucking
embarrassed to ask people for their
personal information on college campuses. I
can remember I actually ran into someone I
knew from high school. I went to school
with her brother. She looked at me like I
had three eyes. She couldn't believe I was
there giving away koozies, pins, and t-shirts.
I came back and I quit.

I felt like a loser. I could not believe I
could not find a job. Did they not know
who I was? Did they not know what I could
do? The answer to both of the questions
was, *no*. They did not know nor did they
care. It was my job to show them what I
could do and what I could become.

At that moment, my wife told me
"You're better than this. Stop limiting

yourself. You have an ability to talk to people and inspire." I knew I needed to change. I didn't need a job, I needed a career. I needed to do something that rewarded me for my hard work and my desire to be the best. A career like that I knew could only be found in sales. The problem with so many sales jobs is people think all sales people are liars and cheaters. I am neither one of those things and I was going to have to prove it.

It was time for me to figure out what the hell I was going to sell to make some real money and take care of my little family.

Chapter 6

Family to Feed

With everything I've done in life, once I make a decision to do it, I go full force. I knew that I was a likable guy and that people found it easy to talk to me. Once I made a career choice in sales, I had no idea what was in store for me. I knew that I could be successful if I put my mind to it, worked hard, and got good mentors.

I went to a job fair, and I found a small independent company that was looking for outside salespeople to do business sales for Nextel. I didn't have any business to business experience, but I did research about the company. I was confident when I went in to talk to the manager. I told him that if he'd give me an opportunity, I'd show him what a good salesperson I could be. I am sure I looked ridiculous in my oversized suit from Foley's but I was there and was bound to be a force to be reckoned with.

When I say outside sales, I really mean outside sales. I was cold calling at office buildings, warehouses, and to anyone that would use our products. I don't care what anyone tells you; that is one of the toughest jobs to have. I am not talking about the door to door salesman that comes to your house to sell you a Kirby vacuum. I am talking about true business to business sales. You make cold calls in person and on the phone. You use your skills to get past the gatekeeper and get to the decision maker. Let me tell you, that's the hardest and best way to cut your teeth in the sales business, because you're told *no* over and over again.

It kind of reminded me of when I was dating Hope. I kept asking her out, she kept saying no, but I wasn't going to take *no* for an answer. We were married and wanted to start a family. I didn't want to live in an apartment. We wanted to buy a townhouse with more room to start a family. This was the first of many homes we would buy over the years, but I would have to say the most gratifying. We were in our mid-twenties and ready to start our lives together in our own home. Hope was a teacher at this point. I've now started my sales career and I wanted to put the effort into it to succeed.

I worked and followed every instruction that my mentor gave me over the course of the next 18 months. I became the most successful outside salesperson in the company. What made me successful was not my product knowledge, but my ability to relate to people. I didn't sit by the phone and wait for it to ring. I was out meeting people and networking. I learned to talk about the things they wanted to talk about, which was usually themselves. I knew I had to get in the car, knock on X number of doors per day, to book so many appointments per week, in order to close so many sales per month. For the first time in my life, I actually started to make some real money. My first full year in the business, I made $40,000. I thought I was crushing it and this $40,000 was going to solve all my problems.

I now had a steady career. I was on my way. Don't get me wrong. $40,000 in the early 2000s was a lot of money. But I was still playing small. At that time, I never would have dreamed of making $40,000 in a month. So many times, we limit ourselves by what we think we can do or what we can't do.

Surround yourself with people that bring out the best in you and help harness your strengths and develop your weaknesses. Surround yourself with people that are going to get behind you and take you to the next level. In this book, I'm going to share with you what took me from making $40,000 a year to making $40,000 a month.

I was in my sales career, and I think I'm crushing it. I was making $40,000 a year. My wife told me, "You know what? You've got opportunity."

My little girl, Alicia, was born on February 19, 2002. She was the most precious thing I had ever seen. At that time, I realized that it was no longer about making little commission checks. This was my little princess, and I was going to buy her whatever she wanted. If she wanted a pony, she was going to get a pony, figuratively or literally. I knew that I had to step up my game. As I mentioned earlier, Hope was a teacher. She was making $40,000 a year. I was making $40,000 year. We thought we were doing well, but I knew deep down inside that she wanted to stay home with our daughter. This was one of the life dreams we discussed in college. It was important for me to be able to do that for her and our family.

With a child comes a new responsibility and we felt we needed more space. We decided to buy our second home, because we now had a family. We went to buy a home in a small brand new community in Richmond, Texas. We encountered a salesperson for new homes in the trailer at the front of the community. This salesperson was an older gentleman who had been in the new home sales business for quite some time. He wasn't a bad salesperson, but was by far not a great salesperson. I remember telling Hope, "Man, if that guy can sell homes and make good money, I could make a fucking killing in this business."

So, I made the decision to get into the new home sales business, because I knew that if this guy could sell homes, I could sell twice as many or three times as many and make more money. In 2003, I was fortunate enough to land a sales position with a very prominent builder in the Houston area. This was one of the largest builders in the US and had a track record of training top notch people. My goal wasn't to sell homes for the rest of my life, but I knew that I had to start somewhere, and I knew that I could be successful in the business.

I was excited. I had found a company that had great training, great mentors, and a great family atmosphere. I realized at that point that it was time for me to start trying to work my way up the corporate ladder. I was focused on promotion even before I started.

When I had my first interview with them, they asked me, "What are your goals here?" I let them know that being a salesperson for the rest of my life was not anywhere on my page of goals. I told them that I knew I had to start somewhere. My goal was to take my entrepreneurial and leadership skills and build a team that made others successful. I was 26 years old, and didn't mind making someone else rich, as long as I was making good money, too.

I got myself ready to run the corporate rat race. I learned here that I am a true reflection of the value I bring to the marketplace. I was competing with people with much more experience than I, for the limited positions up the corporate chain. I knew that I had to bring something different to the table. I knew that I needed to take some action to stand out. Many people believe they have to have everything figured out before they can get the process moving forward. I was a salesperson. What did I do? I took builder classes. I got with my builder, and I learned how to build a house, because I knew the next position up would be managing sales, construction, and warranty. How was I ever going to gain the respect of someone in construction if I didn't know how to build a house? That's why salespeople don't typically get promoted over construction. Most companies' corporate structure consists of a salesman, sales manager, builder, builders' manager, and above them, a division president. In this company, the first level of management was responsible for managing sales, construction, and warranty. They managed the entire P and L for the company. It was a big P and L, with a lot of profit. It was truly an opportunity to run a business, and I wasn't going to let that opportunity slip by. I put in the extra work and took every class that I could find and get into. I also continued to sell homes, because I didn't want to lose the opportunity to advance.

My company had a 12-month training program called the Leadership Program, where we learned from great mentors who helped prepare you for management opportunities. It didn't mean you were going to become a manager. It just meant that if your number was called, you would have that opportunity.

I remember the first day of the class. I was sitting at the Houston office with about 15 other people. Each one of us was at the top of our games and future leaders of the company. The testosterone and egos were high and each person was looking and measuring the other up, thinking *it sucks for you that I will be promoted and you won't.*

Our mentor and trainer for the next 12 months walked in and said, "What do we think of sales people?" He opens the floor up to each person and you hear comments like, "They whine too much," "They don't work hard yet they make all the money." The general consensus was that sales people were prima donnas who made hundreds of thousands of dollars per year and did not earn it.

Then the question of all questions came out of his mouth. "Who here is a sales person?" I was the only person to raise his hand and you could hear a pin drop. You could see their faces turn white like; *oh shit we just let our true feelings be heard.* I was then asked what I thought of builders. I was calculated in my answer. I knew people and I knew this was a test. A true leader does not put someone down to make themselves feel better, but figures out how to bring them up to his level. My answer was simple. "I need my builder. Without my builder it does not matter how many homes I sell if they cannot get built and closed. My builder needs me. It does not matter how many homes he builds. If sales doesn't sell them, he will be out of job sooner than later. Those teams that understand that will thrive and grow."

I earned their respect that day and I think changed the views that some of them had about sales people. I was determined to show them who I was and what I could do. I knew right then I would be getting the spot at the next level and the keys to kingdom.

After 18 months with this company, and 12 months in the Leadership Program, I got called in, and I got promoted. I got promoted to a manager-in-training, meaning I was being groomed to be a manager of my own project. They even put your last name on the project so you know you own it. I worked underneath an existing manager who now had an opportunity to move up the chain even further, to run an entire city.

I ran a small area, typically anywhere between 6 to 10 communities with upwards of 40 people reporting to me. After four to six months of that, I was promoted again to take over my own project. I took a lot of pride in this job. It had my last name attached to it. I was responsible for making my company money. In turn, I would be paid on how well my teams performed ahead of the budget or projections. This was where I excelled. I am great at making other people successful.

I started making over $100,000 a year consistently. We had a nice little life and I was able to buy things that I thought I always wanted. By then, we had two children and Hope was able to stay home with them. Allen was born on August 20, 2007, and my family was complete. I now had both a son and daughter.

I continued to try to move up the corporate ladder. I had people at this company that believed in me and were willing to share their knowledge with me. It was one of the first experiences I had with what I call abundance mentality; meaning that successful people share how they became successful.

That's why I wrote this book. Successful people will share how they've become successful, because they know 95 percent of the people, will never do anything with that information. Successful people, no matter what industry they're in, figure out ways to become successful. This is why people who struggle to find success can never figure out how to become successful. Until you commit to taking imperfect action and working everyday toward your goals, without knowing whether or not it's going to work out, you'll never be successful.

This was a position that I loved. I got to meet families. I got to hire people and run my own business. Then, the mortgage and housing collapse took place. The mortgage meltdown meant builders lost net worth, builders closed down communities, and cities weren't performing. Suddenly, I was staring in the faces of a family that I've got to feed. I wondered, am I next? What was I going to do now?

Living in fear is the worst way to live life. You should never make decisions on the direction of your life when you are scared. You can't always determine if what you see in front of you is a real obstacle or is just in your mind. I was watching people I considered my friends now having to start over in the worst housing market of our times and no one was hiring. I wondered if I had done everything I could to help these folks. I also had to take a hard look at my own life and determine was I prepared if my time in this industry was over.

Chapter 7

Death of My Father

After the mortgage meltdown and the builder crisis, we went from having somewhere in the neighborhood of 30 managers down to 11. I was fortunate enough to make the cut. I attribute a lot of that to aligning myself with the right people. Having mentors in key positions is a great way to ensure your survival in the cut throat game of "Corporate America." I had worked hard. I had made sure that my contributions to the company were noticed. I was consistently making the company millions of dollars per year in profit.

While I was trying to win this corporate rat race and stand out amongst my peers, I wanted to make my father proud and show him that I was successful. My father was always my biggest hero. He was a man of a few words but his love and sacrifice for me was very evident. He pushed me to be the best I could be at everything. His philosophy was if you are going to do it then do it correctly and do it well. I remember as a kid he would never turn me down when I asked him to throw the ball in the back yard or spend time with me. I can honestly say I have not done such a good job with that with my own kids. My career has led to late night phone calls or computer work because my clients want to talk business after they get off of work. Making my dad proud was something I strived for in all aspects of my life, sometimes to no avail.

Then, one night my father went to bed and didn't wake up. This was a shock to my reality and to what I thought was important. I had spent the last six years working extra hard, working weekends, staying late, and trying to be noticed for all the right reasons - because I wanted to make my family proud. I wanted my job security to be there. I wanted my value to be seen. Then my father just went to bed one night and didn't wake up. He died of a heart attack in his own home. I was an only child and now alone to take care of my mom. It was my responsibility to make sure she was going to be OK.

I may have been a man in age but was still a broken little boy when I went to the hospital and heard the words of my mother telling me my father was gone. How could this be? I just talked to him the night before. He was Superman to me. He could not be gone. But as I pulled those partition walls back to stand next to my mother and see my father lying lifeless, my world began crashing down.

When I gave the eulogy at my father's funeral, I wrote down the things that I remembered most about him. The things I wrote down and spoke about in front of our family and friends were not the way I had been living for the last six years. I remembered the sacrifices he had made.

His sacrifices were spending time with me, doing things like playing catch with me when I was a kid. He spent hours and hours at the tennis courts, feeding me tennis balls and sacrificing the items he wanted so I could travel across the country and play in tournaments to be recognized. He did this because he loved me and saw something in me. It wasn't the things that he bought me that mattered. It was the time that he spent with me. He and I took separate career paths. I was a salesperson and an entrepreneur, which meant I worked harder, longer, and faster to make more money. For what? A bigger house? Fancy cars? My father took a simpler route, but was there when I needed him. Now he was gone.

I was in my late 20s, making more money by myself than my parents made combined after 30 years of teaching. I thought that meant I was winning. I was angry when my father died. I was discovering my own mortality. I was beginning to realize that I woke up every day pushing harder and harder and faster and faster, but it really didn't mean anything. Watching my little girl cry at the funeral and looking at my son, who was only one year old and would never know his grandfather, was heartbreaking. Now I could remember the sound of my daughter's voice as I shunned her away time and time again saying, "Daddy's busy. Daddy's on the phone," and her going to her mother and telling her, "Daddy's always on the phone, Daddy's always too busy for me."

It was a reality check when my father passed away and he was no longer there for me to call or ask for advice. That's not the type of relationship I wanted to have with my kids. It was time for me to make a change before it was too late.

Chapter 8

You're Fired

After the death of my father, and the financial meltdown of the mortgage and home building industry, my priorities changed a little bit. Although it was important to me to be successful, how I viewed success needed to change. It was not a big house or a nice car. I had those things. I had had lots of success that many people didn't have in business, but I wasn't having success in life. I had missed birthday parties, sleepovers, and family get-togethers because I chose to work on building an empire of wealth. That's what I thought was expected of me. It was what I thought was important. I put my faith in a company instead of where it really belonged.

After eight years with this company and going from an entry level position to a highly paid manager, I was told that I was going to have the opportunity to be one of the next division presidents and run my own city. Now I was going to make the big bucks. You can imagine that this was a very exciting time for me. I figured my income was going to increase dramatically. We were on the cusp of being able to possibly save money after we bought the nice house and the nice cars.

I continued to fall back into old habits, which was working more and being a company man. I was putting all of my faith in this company instead of where it belonged. I knew that was what I was supposed to do. My family needed me to be more successful, make more money. Or that is at least what I told myself to make myself feel better about being absent from daily family activities.

Some opportunities came and went. I was a loyal employee, drinking the Kool-Aid of Corporate America and being exactly what they wanted me to be. I went and helped with an acquisition of another builder in a different state. I was told there was opportunity and they wanted my input on this new company. After what I believed to be a very successful trip, where we were able to evaluate and analyze the company and the new personnel that would be joining our company and making sure they fit into our culture, I was told I was up for the Division President position there. I didn't get it. The person that got it was an awesome individual. I considered him a friend, and the promotion was well deserved. I just figured my time hadn't come. Unfortunately, after he moved we have not spoken much. That part still bums me out. Looking back, I now see it as an example of how you can think people are your friends, but they are really just coworkers.

Opportunity had come and gone. I was told those weren't the opportunities that I wanted. I was fine with that. I trusted the people above me; my mentors and my company. I had given them my career and I was in their hands to mold. I learned more from these people than I can ever thank them for, but I was still just an employee with someone else controlling my future.

After my father died, I'd confided in some people that I was an only child and that my mom had four strokes at this point. I mentioned that I'd go anywhere I was asked to go, but if there was an opportunity somewhere else in Texas, that'd be great. Then if something happened to my mom, I'd be within a few hours' drive. I heard that opportunities like this existed and I wanted to throw my name in the hat in case there was truth to the rumors. I really wanted this chance. Meanwhile, there was a lot of unrest at home, because we knew that the opportunity meant that we would probably have to move. Moving meant that we would have to leave our home in Houston and start over with no family or friends.

I had learned from some of my mistakes, but I hadn't learned that I was putting my faith in the wrong places. I also hadn't learned that when you work for someone else, you make them rich. At the end of the day, the people that you think are your friends, aren't your friends, they're coworkers. I had created teams of successful people bringing in fantastic results and making the company millions of dollars year after year in profits.

I fully believed at the time that I would retire from this company and would do anything and move anywhere this company asked me to go. Why? Because I was the ideal employee. I did not ask questions. I did what I was told and made the company lots of money.

After bringing another year of success to the company, I was called into the main office while preparing for an annual meeting. At the front desk at the Houston home office, I saw the president of the company walking out of the office of my boss/mentor. He shook my hand and told me to have a nice day. I started to get extremely excited, and thought that I was finally going to get the opportunity I wanted so much. I had heard about something on the horizon and thought, "This must be it!"

I went into the office and sat down with a man who had helped me more than anyone at the company. He was one of my greatest mentors and he always had my back. He looked across the table from me and said, "You're fired." He probably said it a little more politely. I think he said, "We've chosen to go in a different direction." You can understand my total shock and disbelief. I couldn't believe what I was hearing. I thought I was being called in to be promoted. I had worked and sacrificed for this company. I'd done everything that everyone told me to do. I had done what society had told me to do. I thought I was about to get the keys to the kingdom. Instead, I heard, "We no longer want you."

My ego was crushed. In an instant I realized I had misguided loyalty. At this time I didn't even have a LinkedIn account because I didn't want people to think I was showcasing my professional skills to other job opportunities in the market. I realized that we had a business, but the business that I ran was profitable. My teams and people were some of the most successful at the company. Results matter, right?

I was told I was being fired because I had said a curse word that someone overheard and was offended. He said that my language, at times, had bothered people. This was the same company that was run predominantly by men. The use of the word "fuck" was part of everyone's vocabulary, from the top to the bottom.

However, I believe this had more to do with money. I knew that I had made more money than originally anticipated at the beginning of the year. Every year we issued our statements of projected profits for the company and projected bonuses for ourselves. This was not the first time my teams had outperformed the pro forma. I never thought paying me an extra 30k per year would be a problem, since I was making the company an extra 500k.

My mentor could tell I was upset. Since my father had died, he had become more of a father figure to me than a boss. I looked up to him and trusted him. But he couldn't save me this time. He put his hand on my shoulder and said. "Is this the first time you have ever lost a job?" I shook my head; still in disbelief of the news I'd just been given. He calmly said he was proud of me and that I shouldn't worry. He told me I'd be fine, even though it didn't seem like it at that moment. Then he told me that the best was yet to come.

None of that mattered as I sat across that desk. I had to think about how I was going to tell my wife that I no longer had a job. At this time, she's stayed home with our kids for the last few years. I didn't know what I was going to do. How was I going to pay my bills? As I mentioned earlier, I was consistently making well into the six figures. My monthly expenditures were over $10,000 a month. I was now going to have to try to get unemployment, which didn't even cover my house note. How was I going to pay my bills? How was I going to keep our family going?

As I drove home from the office, I called my wife and said, "I've got bad news. I just lost my job." As you can imagine, she was just as astonished as I was. She said, "How's that possible? People like you there.

You've done a great job. You've been loyal."
I said, "I understand, but that's what
happened."

I got home and we talked more about it
and what we were going to do. She was
scared. I could see it in her eyes. She was
looking to me to make it better. I didn't
know how to make it better. All I wanted to
do was get drunk and cry myself to sleep. In
that moment, Hope did exactly what she's
done time and time again. She challenged
me, held me accountable, and reminded me
of who I am.

She said, "You've been home an hour
now. Get your ass off the couch. Get on the
Internet. Start making phone calls. Get on
LinkedIn. Update your resume. Let
everybody know. You've had lots of people
over the years want to hire you. You put

your name out there. We don't sit here and feel sorry for ourselves. We're from the school of get shit done. We are going to make it happen and we're going to be just fine." I looked into her eyes and I believed her.

So, that's exactly what I did.

Chapter 9

Rebirth

Let me tell you, if you've ever been fired from a job, it doesn't take long to figure out who your real friends are. Of all those people that I thought were my friends at my place of employment for almost 10 years, very few checked on me. Very few called. Very few gave a shit.

But my real friends were like my family. They rallied behind me. They surrounded me with love and support and said, "Hey, we don't have a lot, but if you need to borrow money, you can pay me back whenever you get it." I called one of my best friends, a VP at Bank of America who lived in North Carolina, working at their corporate office. He also asked if I needed to borrow money. I have known him since I was 10 years old and he has always had my back. These people saw something in me. They knew that I had been successful and would be successful again. I truly believe that getting to that first $100,000 a year income is the toughest. After that, you can get there time and time again. They believed that I would get there again. Hope knew that I would get there. Therefore, I believed. But let me tell you, starting over at 36 is scary. I was like, "Holy shit."

In the builder world, when you get fired the week before Thanksgiving, nobody's hiring. Every builder in America is finishing out their last fiscal quarter for the fiscal year. Everybody is focused on getting homes completed and closed. Nobody is hiring, I had no idea what I was going to do to feed my family. Hope hadn't worked in years. She could go back to being a teacher, but that wasn't going to support our lifestyle. She looked at trying to get some sort of part-time job, but then I would have to stay home to take care of the kids. If I did that, then I couldn't go to interviews.

So we made a decision. She was going to stay at home, and I was going to look for opportunities. Like I learned before, it's a lot easier to find a job when you have a job. I reached out to my sphere of influence. By this time, I had created a very good sphere of influence of successful people. I was looking at an opportunity with BMW, to go in and start as a salesperson and work my way up. I was also looking at opportunities with other home builders, maybe going back into sales and working my way up. Remember, no one's hiring for high paid managers at this time.

I had a friend who had been in the mortgage business for years. In the past, I had joked with him on more than one occasion that if I ever lost my job, he would need to give me one. He had tried to get me to come into the mortgage business many years earlier. Now he said, "I'll give you an opportunity. You've got connections all over. You know enough to be dangerous." He was willing to give me an opportunity if I wanted to give it a shot. When you have no job and no income, it's a whole lot easier to say, "You know what? I'm going to give this a go. What do I have to lose?"

I had all sorts of doubts. Who was going to follow me? Who was going to talk to me about getting a mortgage? I wasn't a mortgage guy. I was a builder. I knew about profit and loss sheets. I knew about margins. I knew how to motivate and manage people. I didn't know anything about these mortgages, other than we needed one to buy a house. My friend gave me an opportunity, and for that I'll forever be thankful. He went to meetings with me and vouched for me. He would say, "If you give us an opportunity to do the business, I'll make sure that Chad earns more of your business. We'll get these things closed. We're a team."

He paired me up with his production manager, who I sat next to for six months to learn the business. These guys gave me and my family an opportunity when I needed it most. The production manager answered question after questions and looked at every loan I brought in. He will never know how much his time and mentorship meant to me and I truly am proud to call him my friend.

After a couple of loans, I realized I was no longer the new guy. I also learned that the mortgage business is very much about relationships, which is where I excel. I was going to out-work and out-hustle everyone else and get back to where I belonged, which was on top.

Getting on top took a lot longer than I expected. I went 10 months without any sort of real paycheck and I racked up over $50,000 in credit card debt to stay afloat during that time. We cut everything extra out of our life. We did not have money to go out to eat or buy clothes. The hardest thing I had to hear was when my daughter asked me one night, after we canceled all the extras, "Are we poor?" because we told her we couldn't even go to McDonald's with her friends. We did not tell her we were poor. We were not poor. WE WERE BROKE! Poor was a mindset, broke is temporary. My children were very young and I did not want them to feel the pressures of where we were in that stage of our life. They would have plenty of time to stress out about life.

Things got rough and they got rough fast. I remember like it was yesterday. At Christmas time, we couldn't go make gingerbread houses at the local grocery store because we didn't have any money. A woman whose child went to school with our son had heard about our situation. She wanted my kids to be included and offered to pay for them to come and participate in the decorating and then invited us over for dinner. I was so thankful and ashamed at the same time. I was embarrassed that I could not provide for my family the way I always had. I felt like a failure because I was receiving charity from someone my kids went to school with. I wanted to crawl in a hole and die. But I didn't. I went and we decorated and she never made Hope or me feel like we were any different than any of the other families there that day.

Christmas was tough that year. Hope and I received nothing and didn't care, but I was concerned about our kids. I am so lucky that Hope is a planner. I did not know that since we had started the Dave Ramsey plan several months prior, she had been buying our children Christmas gifts all year long, so we wouldn't feel the financial struggle we had so many times before. I know, struggling while making over $100,000 a year makes me sound like an asshole, but the more you make, the more you spend. Our friends and family made sure they picked up the slack where Hope and I needed during that time in our lives. We are very grateful that our kids' memories of those times are limited.

I knew that if I could just stay focused, my time would come, and it would all be worth it. In my first year in the mortgage company, I started to put deals together. I was beginning to make things happen.

Then something crazy happened. In May of 2012, I received a phone call from a recruiter for another builder. It was a builder that I respected and I could see myself working for, so I did a Skype interview. Everything went well. Then they asked me to go meet with the division president in Houston. I went and met with him. He let me know that there were a total of eight candidates.

I believe I went on a total of 4 or 5 interviews. I wanted this job. This job was exactly what I needed and wanted. Remember, I was not a mortgage guy. I was a builder guy who was just stuck doing mortgages until I could get back into the industry. One of the reasons I got into the mortgage business was so I could be close enough if things changed to get back in.

I went to the interviews with laser like focus. I knew my shit. I had made millions of dollars over the years with the previous builder and I knew what this builder was looking for. I studied the company. What they did well, what they didn't and the areas that my experience and expertise could help them achieve the success they were looking for.

They were going to be narrowing it down to two or three candidates for a ride-along. I got through the whole process. I interviewed multiple times over the course of the next few weeks. Remember, making money for a builder is what I spent almost the last 10 years of my life doing. This was something I knew.

I was one of the last three people up for the position when I got a phone call. "Hey, we want you to ride with one of the other managers here. We want to make sure that you're a good fit. We like how things are going, but we're down to three candidates. We're going to make a decision here in the next week."

At this time, I finally thought that it might be a good time to ask about the pay. I found out that the pay would be $10,000 a month salary, plus another $50,000 up for grabs a year in bonuses. The job was $120,000 base salary and $50,000 in bonus, so up to $170,000, which put me right back to where we were with the last company. I ran home to tell Hope, "I'm so excited. I'm going to push so hard to get this job. I'm going to ride along, and I'm going to show them that I'll out-work and out-hustle everybody, and we'll be right back to where we were." At this time, I was on straight commission. I'd been in the mortgage business for four months, and I'd made maybe $8,000 in that time. I was still actually collecting unemployment, because my income was so little and commissioned only. Hope looked at me and said, "I don't think you should take that job."

I remember looking right back at her and saying, "Have you lost your mind? I'm taking this job. This is right up my alley. This is a company that I've heard wonderful things about. This is a company that I told you that I would love to work for. We'll be right back to where we were. We'll have $10,000 a month guaranteed, and we can finally breathe again."

She said, "That management position is being created. What happens if the market doesn't do what they expect it to do? You just lost your job six months ago in that business. You've worked so hard to recreate yourself and build a new brand in a new business. I don't want to see all your hard work go down the drain. Your friend has given you an opportunity, and you're so close."

I said, "Yeah, but honey, we have bills to pay." She said, "I understand. Do me a favor. Talk to some of our closest friends who are successful. Tell them about the opportunity and find out what they think you should do."

Remember, I'm a salesperson, so I had absolute confidence that I could sit down with each of these people and explain to them the feature benefit. The feature is I've got bills to pay. The benefit of this job is that it gives me money to pay my bills. This was not going to be a tough sale for me.

I sat down with one of our closest friends, who is a general manager at a BMW store. She was also the maid of honor in my wedding and one of my wife's oldest and dearest friends. I told her how excited I was, and explained to her why I should take this job and how it was going to get me back. I told her how we were struggling to pay bills and needed some security again because I needed to get back on top. Hope had not signed up for this and the stress of making no money was wearing thin on both of us. She knew what I had been through and how I was able to build teams and make companies lots of money. She had even offered me an opportunity with her company to work my way up. It was an honor that she would consider hiring me with such a great company with such great earning potential and that made the decision that much tougher.

Then, I sat down with one of my other best friends, who owns a dental practice. He and I have talked a lot about business and money over the years. I trusted him. I opened up about how scared I was and that I felt liked like a failure and a sucker for putting all my faith in a company that did not have the same loyalties I had given to them. I was able to bear my soul about where I was in life and that I was scared.

This alone for me was difficult. I came from a family that loved each other very much but we did not talk about our feelings in that way, especially with people outside of the family. I was ready to present my case and so I went through the same scenario with him. I told him how excited I was, and all the reasons I should take this opportunity. I told him how the money was desperately needed and would get us back on track. He knew the feeling of failure and that the lack of money coming in was causing problems in my marriage. Money is the number one reason people fight in marriage and at this time Hope and I had none.

Then, I sat down with a third close friend, who is manager of a large national crane company. I shared many of the same stories and feelings. I knew they all needed to know where I was mentally and emotionally to be able to give me the best advice. I was confident I knew the advice they were going to give me too.

I sat down with all three of these people, and I told them that we are $50,000 in debt and that we didn't have enough money to pay our bills. I said, "I asked for your opinion because I trust and respect you. You know how hard things are right now for our family. We can't pay our bills for the first time in our lives. We are using credit cards to stay afloat. We are scared, tired and ready to put this nightmare behind us."

Then something crazy happened. Just when I thought I had given the best sales presentation of my life, not one of those people said, "You should take the job."

They said, "Chad, you've been working so hard to build up something for yourself. Last hired could be first fired. I'm sure you'll be successful there, but do you really want to go back to Corporate America, where you put all your faith, and then one day got called in and told, "You're fired?"

I couldn't believe what I was hearing. Had they not been listening? I was BROKE and SCARED! But here's what I knew. I knew that if God wanted me to move forward on my journey as an entrepreneur, there was a bigger reason, and I needed to listen. I went home to discuss with Hope what I had just heard from some of our closest friends. I asked her to sit down and listen while I went over detail after detail of how my conversations went and what advice I had received. I was still in shock.

She smiled. You know, the kind of I told-you-so smile. She believed in me when I was at my lowest and in my darkest times. They say you can tell a lot by a man's character not by how he handles himself in good times but how he handles himself I bad times. In the middle of a shit storm you will learn who your real friends are, who is there with you through thick and thin and who loves you unconditionally. We talked for about an hour and then we made the decisions together like we had done every other time in our lives.

So I picked up the phone, begrudgingly, and I called the division president. I said, "I want to thank you for the opportunity of getting down to the last three, but I'm afraid I'm going to have to remove myself from consideration." I felt that it was better to remove myself instead of waiting until they offered me a job and I had to decline it because it wasn't the right decision. He asked me if I was sure. To be honest, I was not sure at all. If I could just see beyond the horizon, all the work I had put in was about to explode.

These people and their families are my family now and I would do anything I could to help them just like they helped me so many years ago. Build your team strong and they will lift you up when you fail and hit adversity.

Chapter 10

The Vultures of Opportunity

I had passed on a $150,000 to $170,000 a year job. What the hell was I going to do? I still had plenty of doubts but I was all in at this point. What I did was get off my ass and put imperfect action into place. I started hustling and grinding every day, knowing that it was totally up to me. My paycheck was going to be based on the value I brought to the marketplace. I was going to go out and show everyone that I was going to make it in this business. I was not only going to make it, I was going to fucking CRUSH it!

Like I said in in a previous chapter, there are people out there working twice as hard to take your shit - your clients, your money and your reputation. Along with success comes people that are out to either use you for their own good or to take it from you.

I've just decided that I'm not going to take a safe job and follow in my parents' footsteps. I was going to give this career as a mortgage originator 150 percent of my effort, because I knew that the success was just beyond the horizon. I went from making $8000 in the first five months of the year to making over $100,000 a year the last six months of the year.

I had aligned myself with a friend who had given me an opportunity to be successful. I was not going to waste the opportunity he gave me. I was not going to let him down. He did as he promised. He delivered on everything he said he was going to do. He put me in a position to be successful with supporting operations behind me. I was able to go out there and do what I do best, which is build relationships and sell. He made sure the loans I brought in closed and closed on time. He even put some of his own loans on the back burner to make me look good. He knew I was fighting for my life here and was going to fulfill his promise from all those years earlier.

Putting imperfect action to the test, I got out there every day, and did something towards the success of my future. I joined networking groups. I went to network happy hours. I started using my sphere of influence to my advantage. I reached out to people I knew in the business as Realtors and builders. My first big break came with a friend I had hired many years earlier at the builder I used to work for. He was an amazing sales person and a great human being. He had become a Sales Manager with a builder here in Houston. I reached out and asked him for the opportunity to sit down and pitch to him why I deserved his business. This connection proved to be the spring board to my business. How many of you reading this never think to utilize the people in your own back yard? These people know you and trust you, yet you don't ever contact them to help you grow.

115

Know this; if you fuck it up, it is worse because they trusted you. I was able to close this account and meet some great people along the way. I am still the preferred lender for this builder today as I write this book.

In 2013, I really started to catch my stride. I was picking up new referral partners and venturing out with new builders. Builder business was easy for me. I knew their lingo. I knew what was important to them. Hell, I was one of them pretending to be a loan originator. But this is when things really changed for me. I was able to take a relationship I had grown and landed a new builder that was growing, and growing fast. I landed a major builder that we took from just one community to up to 60 percent of the city, by delivering and doing what we said we were going to do. We closed loans quickly and efficiently, we called customers back, and did all the basic 101 mortgage things that so many lenders over the years had forgotten. I got into the mortgage business at the end of 2011. At the beginning of 2012, when the economy was still shit, people weren't buying homes. The housing market and the mortgage business still had a blemish. But that didn't stop me. I knew that if I leveraged the relationships and I worked harder than anyone else, my business would grow.

My second year in the business, things really started to get going. As a second year guy, I continued to build and hustle, and I closed over $18 million. My first full year in the business was over $100,000, but by my second year, my income soared to over

$200,000. I was no longer worrying about money. I was able to start paying down debt and put money away for a rainy day.

I heard a saying once, "it's not if it's going to rain, it's when it's going to rain." I had already been through a storm, and I didn't want to go through that again. But one problem in the mortgage origination business is that when you start to have success, people start coming out of the woodwork to tell you how they can help you. The vultures of opportunity started to call and want me to work with them. That was a huge struggle for me, because my friend had given me an opportunity when I needed it, and I'm a loyal person by nature. For months after months, I would turn down those advancements, saying, "No, I'm perfectly happy here," because I was. "I'm not looking for another opportunity," because I wasn't. Money was good. The company was good. The team environment was good. I was very happy.

But as my business continued to grow, I realized that there was opportunity out there. Then, I felt like it was my obligation to at least hear what that opportunity looked like. I owed it to my family, and I owed it to myself. Just two years earlier, my loyalty had cost me my career. As much loyalty and respect I had for my friend, I had learned that at the end of the day I had to do what was best for Chad and his family. I had to make some tough decisions. I started meeting with other companies to find out which direction I wanted to go.

I knew that based on the amount of production that I had, opening up my own branch was an opportunity that I wanted to take. It was a chance for me to create something for myself and my family. I was very fortunate that I had multiple companies want to meet with me and many others that I didn't meet with, simply because I didn't feel like we clicked over the phone. I was very fortunate to get five written offers from companies doing $100 million a year to companies doing $5 billion a year.

When I met with these companies, I realized many of them were only worried about what I could do for them. They wrote up these wonderful offers. They stated things like, "By month three, you'll have two loan officers. By month six, you'll have four. By month nine, you'll have six. By month 12, you'll have 10. We're going to be doing $10 million a month. Yes, you'll be making $300,000 a year, but this is what you're going to do for me."

Then something funny happened. After I'd already narrowed my choices down to about four or five companies, I got a call from a small local mortgage company in Sugar Land, Texas. A mutual friend had referred me to them because he knew that I was possibly looking. A gentleman there said "I hear you might be interested in opening up your own branch. We're looking for like-minded individuals to open up a branch in the area that you're interested in. Could we sit down and have lunch?" By this time, I'd already taken about eight months to figure out what I was going to do, because I felt very loyal to my friend. But I knew a change had to be made. I went to lunch with the Owner, the COO, and the Senior Vice President. We all clicked. They asked me my time frame. I explained to them that I had over four and a half million dollars closing in December and I would not be making any decisions until January of the following year. Basically, I told them to "Reach out to me later."

This meeting took place in October. I went about my business closing loans and not thinking much about it. By December, I had already made the decision to go somewhere else, because I hadn't heard anything from this company, which was weird. I told my wife, "We had such a great meeting. I thought we hit it off. I'm not sure where they went."

About a week before Christmas, I got a call from the Senior Vice President who said, "Hey, Chad. Haven't talked to you in a few months. Just want to make sure that you're still interested." I said, "That's funny, because I hadn't heard from you guys. I thought y'all weren't interested." His response was, "You told us you weren't moving until January and not to bug you. The last thing I wanted to do was stalk you during the busiest month of your year." Then he asked me to please not make any decisions until we got an opportunity to meet for lunch. I agreed and we met the next day.

I went in and I met for lunch with them again. Afterwards, I went back to the corporate office. The owner of the company asked me to write down all the things it was going to take for me to come work for them. I had five other written offers. I'd already kind of decided a place but hadn't verbally committed. So, I just wrote down the best things of each of the 5 offers, thinking, "There's no way in hell they're going to do this." I went home and told Hope that the meeting went well and I probably just cost myself the opportunity because I just swung for the fences. I felt I had nothing to lose at the time as I was making good money and had already in my mind picked another place. It wasn't that I did not want to work there but I felt like it would be easier to justify why I did not get the offer because of the things I wanted.

To my surprise, I got a call the next morning at 9:00 from the owner of the company. He said, "We agree to all of these terms. When can you start?" Suddenly, I thought, "Holy shit." I started crawfishing because it's not what I expected. I said, "You know, me and my wife, we make decisions together. Because I told you, she's been with me through thick and thin. She's always encouraged me and believed in me, even when I didn't believe in myself."

He said, "You know what? We think that's great. My wife and I, we make all our decisions together as well. What is your wife doing tomorrow for lunch? We'd like to have her come to lunch with us. We're an open book here, and she can ask us any question that she wants."

There was no getting out of that one. The next day, we went to lunch. My wife got a chance to ask some questions, and they got to ask her a few questions. I told you before, Hope is a smart woman. Unlike me, she very rarely puts her foot in her mouth or shows all of her cards before she makes a decision. She sat there very intently and processed all the information. At one point during lunch you could tell her calm demeanor was worrying them. They asked, "How are we doing? We aren't sure if this is going well because you are so quiet." She explained to them she listens and processes information differently but she supports me. What is funny is we deal with sales people all day who don't know when to stop talking and let the process take its natural course. My wife, on the other hand, has the patience of Job and is able to evaluate very clearly what she wants to accomplish.

As we were leaving after lunch, my wife turned to me and said, "That's where you need to go. That's where you fit. That's exactly what you were looking for."

Now, I faced two of the toughest decisions of my career: Where was I going to go to open up a branch, and how was I going to tell my friend, who had given me an opportunity when I needed one? I had been driving over an hour one way to the office at my previous companies for years. I was spending thousands of dollars on gas and tolls, not to mention the wear and tear on my car. I was determined to get myself a little closer to home.

Now what to say to my friend was the next thing I needed to figure out. My friend had given me an opportunity when my family had nothing. I had to muster all my courage up to go in and tell him I was quitting so I could chase another dream.

Chapter 11

Death of My Mother and My Career...Not If I Have Anything To Do With It

The year was 2014. This was going to be the best record year of my career. I was finally opening up my own branch, and I was going to be able to call all the shots. With opening a branch, there were a lot of new challenges to be faced, but the financial reward was unparalleled. I was not only responsible for bringing in the business but I was in control of my own operations. I had hired an amazing processor and a production manager to help me with my business.

I had spent the past two years building my business around a large home builder here in Houston. This builder was doing a couple hundred closings a year, and I was doing approximately 60 percent of the entire city. I had built my entire business to be a seamless transition for their company. Their account was the main reason I was able to have enough business to open up my own branch. Once I got settled into 2014, I was staring at a pipeline of about seven million dollars in closings over the course of the next four months.

This type of business makes it very easy to forecast your income, but also comes with a price. The price that comes from having an account like this is it often takes up a lot of your personal time, which means you spend less time with friends and family. I actually didn't coach my son's flag football team because I felt like I needed to be available to answer the phone when this builder's sales and clients called. This is one of the regrets I have most about putting my career before my family again, but I'll talk more about that later.

Financially, things were starting to really take off for me. I had now been able to pay down the approximately $50,000 debt that I had incurred while I was unemployed. The opportunity of having my own branch gave me the chance to make more money. I was also able to start saving, which I hadn't been able to do in years. I was bound and determined to not let the mistakes of my past be the mistakes of my future, meaning I was not going to put my career in anyone else's hands. I was not going to put myself in a position where, if I fell on hard times, or if things got slow, I couldn't pay my bills because I had no money. I was determined to not live check to check. I was also determined to try to be a better man for my family. Unfortunately, I found out that when you reach a certain level of success, you're pulled in multiple directions. You become addicted to the money and the things that money can buy.

In May of 2014, my life would be rocked, not only professionally, but also personally. The first week of May started out like any other week of the month. I was getting prepared for my monthly meeting with my builder to go over closings for that month. This was something that I had done for the last two years. I always looked forward to the meetings, because I was able to figure out who we needed to start locking in, how much revenue would be generated, and whether or not we were going to have a good month.

This month had started off a little bit differently. My mother informed me that she had been to the doctor because she was concerned she had cancer. She had been complaining about stomach discomfort for a few months but did not think much about it. She had four strokes over the years but cancer was never anything she really ever talked about or was scared about. It did not really run in the family so it was not the first thing that came to mind when the pain and discomfort started happening.

After multiple trips to the doctors and specialists, our worst fears were confirmed. They found a tumor the size of a softball in her body. Just as my financial world was going strong, I was now being kicked in the stomach with the reality that my mom was facing the battle of her life. I knew she was scared. I could hear it in her voice when we spoke. I was scared too, but I tried to not let her know and tried to sound positive.

As I was trying to figure out how to cope and prepare for my meeting, all of the thoughts of what was important came rushing back to me. How did I forget the lessons I had learned when my father passed? A certain level of success brings a certain level of blindness, as well.

I found out on Monday, May 3rd, that my mother was diagnosed with appendix cancer. On Tuesday, I went to my meeting, still groggy with the news I had just received. As I sat down with the manager like I did every month, I could see that something was different in his eyes. He knew the type of risk I had taken with opening my branch, and that they were the main component I had structured my business around. We sat there in the restaurant, having coffee like we had so many times before. It was the day after I found out that my mom was going to be fighting for her life. That's the day he told me that they had decided to open up their own mortgage company, and that my services would no longer be required.

Then it hit me. My mother was going to have to fight for her life, and I just lost a $15 to $18 million a year account. 80 percent of my business just walked right out the door. I didn't know what I was going to do. I had to figure out how I was going to replace the business.   More importantly, I had to figure out what I was going to do to help my mother. My mom and I always had a special relationship. I was, for a lack of a better term, a momma's boy. We talked on the phone every day and she went to dinner with me and the family at least once a week, if not more. We knew time was of the essence.

We immediately got my mom in to have surgery, and after that, started the chemo and radiation. If you've ever been with a family member who is battling

cancer, and going through chemo and
radiation, you know that it is very difficult
to watch the person that you love
deteriorate right in front of your eyes. I had
witnessed this many years earlier, with my
mother-in-law, as she battled breast cancer.
I now had to face this with my own mom.
When my dad passed away, it was very
different. My dad went to bed one night
and didn't wake up. He died of a heart
attack due to what I believe was from a
blood clot from back surgery he had a few
months earlier. I can argue with you on
both sides of the coin which one is easier.
Would I rather have the opportunity to say
goodbye, at the same time watching her go
through this battle, knowing that there is
only so much I can do to help? It was a huge
challenge for me. I still struggle with it

today. I miss her today and it makes me sad that my children will grow up without their grandparents.

Over the course of the next five months, I was trying to figure out a way to replace my business and be the son that I knew I needed to be. This is an area that I believe I failed in greatly. I was fortunate enough that I had Hope and other family members that came to help take care of my mom because I was truly drowning at this stage in my life. Hope and I tried to get my mom to move in with us, but that was something that she said she didn't want to do. Looking back, I can say that I understand that, because she wanted to go through this battle in her own home where she was comfortable, and where she and my father had lived. But I still felt like I was being an inadequate son.

Not only was I dealing with the struggles that were going on with my mom, I was now trying to figure out how to replace all the business that I had lost. Although I was hurting personally, I was also beginning to hurt financially again. I knew that if I didn't replace this business, I could find myself in the same spot I was just a few years earlier. I was angry because of all the hard work I had put in, and wondered why I wasn't getting the breaks that other people were getting. Why was it that I had to deal with loss? Why did I have to start over again?

Life can be a real bitch and it takes many people down with it. I was determined to not be a casualty. If you are struggling to find a way to make it, just look around at your *whys* and remember that is all worth it and get your nose back to the grindstone and make it happen. You are stronger than you know. It is times like these that I have been both my strongest and my weakest at the same time.

I now had to come to grips that the reason that Hancock Mortgage Partners, were extremely excited to have me was based on that large account. I had to go and tell the owners and the senior executives that I knew they had brought me on with the expectation of all these closings from this builder, and now that business was gone.

I was emotionally and physically broken with what my mother was going through, and what I was trying to do to rebuild my business again. My mom continued to fight over the next few months like the brave woman she was. She did not complain and did everything she could to fight this vicious disease. She was so ill that she could not eat. The pain she was in was unbearable and seeing the pain in her face and hearing it in her voice made me want to cry like a child and pretend it wasn't happening. But it was happening and we were witnessing it firsthand. I would go to the doctors' appointments, along with my aunt and uncle, who had been taking turns to care for her. Maybe I was naïve or foolish but I believed in my heart of hearts that she was going to be ok. We had a plan and we were going to execute that plan.

That planned never came to fruition. The disease and the chemotherapy ate through her body with a vengeance. Then my mom passed away in mid-August 2014. I cannot describe to you how I felt when I received the phone call from my uncle telling me I needed to get there quickly. I knew something wasn't right. I was supposed to have lunch with her the next day, and that day never happened. I would encourage you to spend time with your loved ones, because you never know when something may happen and that person is taken away from you.

I now had to figure out how to battle the demons inside of me that were telling me to give up. As a child, when I envisioned how my life was going to be, I never imagined that by the time I turned 38 years old I would have lost my mother and my father. With no brothers and sisters to help carry the burden, I was now a 38 year old orphan. I had watched my mother fight like crazy for her life, and there was no way that I was going to lose my mother and my career in the same year. I made a commitment to not give up.

When you go through tragedies in life, whether they're personal or professional, you find out who your real friends are. You find out where you rank with your family. You find out who talks about you behind your back, and who supports you both verbally and in the shadows.

I found out many of these things when my mom passed. I can honestly tell you I don't believe that I have the best relationship with my family. It's not because they don't love me or I don't love them. But we've never been a family that's great on communicating what's important. When you grow up living so far away from each other and everyone has their own life, extended family becomes less of a priority. I realized they were battling their own grief during this process. I don't blame anyone for how they felt. I'm still angry that I lost both of my parents. I still feel like it's not fair. But I refuse to let it break me and keep me down.

You have choices in your life. You can either let life control you, dictate you, and tell you how you're going to feel, or you can take control of your own life, get up, put in the work and make things happen. I share this story, as hard as it is for me to write it, because I have reached the pinnacles of success, and I have reached the depths of despair more than once in my life. Those who truly believe that they are destined for greatness, and are willing to do anything they can to be successful, have an obligation to themselves and their family. My wife and my two children are my *why*. They're why I get up every day and push so hard. If you don't know what your *why* is, you will be unhappy no matter how much money you make or stuff that you buy. You have read many times in this book how I have put my career ahead of my family. Sometimes because I thought that is what I had to do to be able to provide for them. We live in a funny world where we must work to live the life we want to live but if we work too much we miss the life we tried to create.

Death of My Mother and My Career...
Not if I Have Anything to Do With It

In the course of six months, I had witnessed my mother pass and my career crumble. Now I'm starting over again.

Chapter 12

You Have To Get Off Your Ass If You Plan To Be Rich

After my mother passed away in August of 2014, I had to figure out what I was going to do to rebuild my business and get my life back together. Things for me had always come easy, meaning that on every career path I'd ever started I had been able to work my way up. I'd always been able to make connections and build relationships with people. But after two career blows and the deaths of my parents, who had supported me and unconditionally loved me, I was definitely feeling lost. I thought about giving up.

We all need to have those *whys*, why we get up in the morning, why we work so hard and why we push ourselves. Those *whys* for me are my wife, Hope, and our two children, Alicia and Allen. You need to find your *why*, if you're ever going to make it through the thick of the storm. Your *why* has to be greater than your *can't*. I couldn't give up because my *whys* are so important, so I had to figure out a way to reinvent my business. I started in this business a few years earlier, without this home builder, and had done just fine. It was my mistake that I had put all my efforts into building my business around a partner who wasn't truly a partner. I was determined to not make that mistake again. I didn't know exactly how I was going to do it, but just like many times before, I knew that as long as I took imperfect action, set goals and worked towards those goals every day, I would be successful again. I had done this time and time again in my career and in my personal life, and had seen the results.

This decision to take back my business did not happen right after my mom died. It actually happened a few months before she passed. I knew she was not getting better, but I remained optimistic. I was also fighting the demons that told me I wasn't a good son, while watching my mom deteriorate down to 67 pounds from cancer and chemotherapy. Meanwhile, I still had to work and bring in business, because there were bills that had to be paid.

Many of us spend a lot of time on social media, whether it's Instagram, Twitter, Snapchat or Facebook. I was just like anyone else, and felt like it was just a mindless tool. I'm able to sit there at various times of the day when I'm stressed out, see what's going on, and not have to think about the responsibilities that I have. One day, a very unique thing happened. I saw a video from an Internet marketer/sales coach come across my screen. What made this video different from any of the other scrolling ads I had seen in my news feed was that he was very similar to me in the sense that he was very dynamic, very passionate, and had an in-your-face attitude that said "it's up to you to be successful." He was telling it like it is, and said if you didn't like where you were in life, to get off of your ass and make shit happen. On more than one occasion, I had functioned on this same methodology to be successful and make others successful.

You've read many times in this book how I didn't necessarily know where I was going, but I knew I had to get off of my ass if I was ever going to make anything of myself. I knew it was totally up to me. No one was going to come and save me; not my parents, not my family, not my friends, not my government. It was all up to me. I learned that I was the only one holding myself back, and I could achieve anything that I put in front of me, if I just put in the work. I had never been afraid of work. What

I needed was someone to point me in the right direction, and that's what I got.

I realized that there was an entire world of untapped clients and potential that I was not even hitting. When I met Ryan Stewman for the first time in 2014, it was not in person, or in a Facebook chat. It was in an ad, directed right at me. The ad stated, "If you're a loan officer, and you're not making at least $20,000 a month, you're a fucking loser, and you should go work at the mall and be ashamed of yourself." But if I wanted to know how to go from $20,000 to $40,000, he was the guy to call.

I realized that I was his perfect client. I had been making $20,000 a month. I was happy and the bills were paid. I had re-established myself. Now I had just lost a $15 million to $18 million a year account, and I had to figure out what I was going to do next. Once all those closings in my pipeline closed, it was game-on time. I clicked on the ad, because I was intrigued and I wanted to get more information. I didn't know that this was going to open up a whole new world for me. What I mean by this is it reevaluated my understanding of what a life of abundance meant.

What I learned at that moment was there was an untapped market in social media advertising that I was missing. I was determined to figure out a way to make it a part of my business plan. I was confident that with the right tools, my business would skyrocket. Now it was up to me to take the time to learn all the new ways to bring value to the marketplace. I knew the days of donuts and rate sheets were dead. I started watching sales videos and learning the techniques of internet marketing. I was becoming a marketing ninja, producing new business with my new-found skills.

I landed a custom home builder here in Houston using one of the social media techniques that I learned in a free webinar, and started implementing other free content and sales strategies. Maybe I knew what to do, maybe I just lost focus, or maybe I just needed someone to tell me to get in there and do the fucking work. After four months, my business started to thrive again. I started reestablishing past relationships with Realtors and referral partners. I started generating new relationships. My thought was, if the free stuff was working this well, what did the paid stuff offer?

I didn't know what I was going to do, and how much I was going to spend, but I knew if I didn't invest in myself and my business, who would? My company had got behind me when I first started, said that they believed in me, and gave me an opportunity to own my own branch. It was up to me to fulfill my end of the bargain.

I clicked back on an ad and I filled out the form for more information. I knew it was time to hire a coach. I remember receiving that phone call and being asked if I was willing and committed to putting in the work. It was one of the strangest sales calls I have ever been on. Here I am, a salesperson, getting a sales call from someone, knowing that I'm not going to get sold, but I just wanted to find out more information. I heard what was offered, and that his belief system was right in line with mine. Right after we talked, I knew that there was a connection. We discussed how I could bring value to the marketplace. I said, "I do loans." He said, "OK, and so do thousands of other people. How do you truly bring value to the marketplace? Your paycheck is a direct reflection of the value that you bring to the marketplace."

I knew that I brought value. I didn't know how much, or when, or where. I learned to not limit myself. I was held accountable again and all I needed to do was to take my knowledge, relationships, and experience to a whole new level. I knew truly the only way that I could bring value to the marketplace was to offer up something to my referral partners that they needed most. When you're in real estate, the thing that you need most is leads. I realized that I needed to learn how to generate and create leads, because if I was able to generate and create leads for my referral partners, I would separate myself from every other loan officer in my market, because no one is giving out leads on a consistent basis. They may give out their cousin, or their brother, or their friend down the street to a Realtor, but there are only so many of those. If you're working with 20 to 30 Realtors, chances are you're not going to be able to generate 20 to 30 leads a year to give to each one of them one. I knew that by being able to provide leads to my referral partners, I was going to change the way the game was played. I was going to have to outwork, outlearn and out implement through imperfect action and figure out a way to incorporate a system to generate business for my referral partners.

Today I give out between 70 and 90 leads every week to my referral partners, but more on that later.

Chapter 13

Freedom

Once I figured out how to create value in the marketplace by generating purchase referral leads for my referral partners, my business blew up. It went to a whole new level. Now, I was the one in control. I was the one able to set where I wanted to go. Now, I had to figure out a way to get myself out there and be noticed. I had to take my business and my brand an up a notch.

I focused on personal branding. I wanted to make sure that my face and my message was in front of my perfect client. I wanted to make sure that I was the one they thought of when they needed a mortgage or they needed to grow their business. I started doing all sorts of things that were outside of my comfort zone. I started having intent purpose through social media. I began to add people that I didn't know on a daily basis. I figured the more people I was in front of, the more exposure I would generate by getting in front of their friends, and their friends, and their friends. I'd be able to create a syndicate of people and advertising that would be taking place 24 hours a day, with or without me.

I knew that I had to stay relevant. I knew that had to put out good content. It had to be information that people wanted. I started creating videos called Fun-Fact Friday, where I would tell people information that they needed to know to buy a house in 2015. 2015 for me was going to be the year I created the brand of Chad Prior. Yes, I was a mortgage guy, but I was going to become THE mortgage guy. My videos were starting getting more and more views. Now my videos get anywhere from 1000 – 2000 views within a week. These videos were being watched by all the people that would benefit from the content I was providing.

I was looking to generate a business, based on relationships and value in the marketplace, and a brand that people could trust and know. That is what I've been able to do. Not only have I been able to create a brand for myself, but I've been able to create a brand for all the loan officers that work for me as well. I then took it a step further and now teach my referral partners how to create their brand on social media.

Facebook currently has over 1 billion users. When Alexander Graham Bell invented the telephone there were approximately 1 billion people on the planet. Now that many people are on Facebook. There is an untapped market of potential clients and referral partners right at your fingertips waiting to be connected with.

What happens when you take imperfect action and you get out there and you create something that creates and generates buzz and lights on like fire? You no longer have to go out and hunt and beg referral partners to do business with you. There is no more "Here's your rate sheet, here's your donuts. Can I have your business?" You now have something of value.

What I was able to do was turn one or two leads a week into 70 to 90 leads a week for my referral partners. I was building a brand on Facebook. Now, Realtors see what I'm doing and who I'm working with and reach out to me and say, "Hey how do I become part of that program?"

Here's what I tell them, "My goal is to give you a minimum of five potential purchase referral leads a month. That's 60 a year. If you are able just convert 10 percent of those, that's six more closings this year than you had last year. At an average sales price of $300,000, I just put $54,000 in your pocket. Did your current lender put $54,000 in your pocket last year?" We know the answer to that is no or they wouldn't be sitting there talking to me, they wouldn't be reaching out to me asking how to become part of the program.

Then I was able to take this program a step further. Remember, I told you I had to fulfill and replace $15 million to $18 million. Instead, I exceeded that. I was able to grow my branch. This is where it got really exciting, because when other loan officers started to see the work I was putting in, they would hit me up on Facebook and ask me questions. The last three loan officers that I've hired actually reached out to me and said. "Hey, I want to come work for you." Now, they don't have to go out and be the "here's your rate sheets and here's your donuts" type of loan officer. I'm teaching them how to become professionals in their industry. I'm providing them platforms that help generate more business for them and their referral partners. I'm teaching them how to go out and get referral partners, how to establish those relationships and how to bring value. I'm helping them achieve financial goals and financial success levels that they never thought were possible.

That's where it gets really exciting. Being in control of your own destiny and working with like-minded individuals is very exciting. I now get to pick and choose the Realtors and the relationships that I want to have because I have something of value. I'm able to teach this to the people that work with me. I'm able to help lift them. Just as my mentors did for me, I understand that if I take care of them and help them reach their personal and professional goals, I will create a team that is so powerful that there's nothing we can't accomplish.

In this book I've talked about success in business, and I've talked about success in life. I've talked about failures in business, and I've talked about failures in life. At the end of 2011 when I lost my job and wasn't sure what I was going to do, I never would have dreamed that I would have been able to reach the financial success and freedom that I've been able to reach today. Just four years ago, I was unemployed with no direction. In the last three years I have been able to achieve financial security for myself and my family by building a business, a brand and a system to help my referral partners and my loan officers grow their business.

I was taught a long time ago that it's not about me, it's about them. I lost sight of that. If you focus on living a life of abundance and helping others, everything that you want, you will receive.

Like any good story, there have to be lessons that have to be learned. Although I've been fortunate enough to reach financial security over the past three years, I didn't go out and start buying crazy things. I didn't go out and buy vacation homes and boats and things of that nature. I learned from the mistakes of my past. I surrounded myself with good people. I believe that you're an average of the five people you hang out with most. I learned that it was an obligation to myself and my family to diversify. I started diversifying my assets and looked at other business opportunities. My wife and I started doing house-flipping and rentals. We paid off our vehicles because I knew that I could fall on hard times just as easily as I'd become successful, in fact, probably even easier. I wanted to make sure that, if at any given time my success stopped or halted in any way, I was not going to be the same person I was in 2011. I wasn't going to be living check to check, with no money in the bank, car payments, house payments, bills out the wazoo and not knowing what I was going to do. I learned from the past mistakes that I've made. I'm excited that I'm able to teach other people to be everything that they want to be and how not to make the same mistakes. We started diversifying. We started saving our money again and investing in ourselves.

As before, all of this success brings the vultures of opportunity. My company recognized the value I was bringing. I was approached in 2015 to teach and take over other branches around the country and show them how to build their business through social media, marketing, self-branding, and providing leads and value to their referral partners. The owner, the chief operating officer and the senior vice president asked me to go to lunch. At that lunch they asked me if I would be interested in becoming part of their corporate team, and teaching this to other people.

If you remember from earlier chapters, I had put a lot of faith in organizations before, only to be disappointed to the level that I lost my job and missed out on opportunity after opportunity over the years. In our world, the value I bring to the marketplace is how my paycheck is determined. I knew that it was not in my best interest to go sit on the 10th floor of the beautiful glass building down the street and give up on my relationships in order to teach others. I have an abundance mentality now; a very different mentality. When they asked if this is something that I wanted to do, I kindly declined that opportunity because I knew in my world the real money made is in the production of business. That's something that no one can take away from me because these are my clients and my referral partners.

This company did something that was so unexpected. They believed in me. It's actually one of the reasons I wrote this book. They believed in me two years earlier when I came to them by myself to open up a branch with no additional loan officers, no processors, and no underwriters. Then I had a great big account and I lost that account within two months joining the company. When I went to these three men and I said, "I know you hired me because of this home builder account but they've decided to open up their own mortgage company. I don't know what I'm going to do." All three of them looked at me and said, "We don't care about that builder. We hired you for you. We saw something in you that was different. We believe in you."

As I sat there at the table listening to their new offer, I didn't want to disappoint them by telling them I wasn't interested. At the same time, I had to look out for me and my family. I didn't want to create this environment, show everyone what I was doing and then have it taken away from me. Then, this company did something that I couldn't believe. They believed in me, but they didn't steal my value. They increased it. I have a mentor here at this company who I consider a friend who has guided me on many big decisions over the last couple years. He told me that he believed in "biggest and best use". My biggest and best use was to build relationships and originate loans. He has a favorite phrase, "You don't put the car in front of a racehorse." It sounded funny the first time I heard it, but as I've spent more time around him and watched how he's developed and grown people and our company over the years, it makes perfect sense. The owner of our company said, "I've got a deal for you. How about we create something together that would be mutually beneficial for you and us? We will make your life easier. We'll help manage it and run it. You get to still have all the credit." I couldn't believe what I was hearing.

Up until this point everything they had delivered on had exceeded my expectations. I felt there was no reason not to trust them but I did have to question whether or not what they said was real, because of my past experiences. I expressed my concerns to my mentor. I had to make a decision to let go of something that I built and allow them to make it even better.

One thing I can tell you is when you start marketing yourself and generating leads for your referral partners and doing all the work that other people aren't doing, there are only so many hours in the day and they needed to be done more efficiently. That's what my company was able to do for me as they took what I did and we put it on steroids.

We have been able to take our lead generation to a whole new level and can bring on branches and loan officers and help supplement their business and help them bring more value to their referral partners.

Now we pump out 1,000 leads a month to our referral partners all around the country.

There is no more power in this business than to be able to tell a Realtor or a loan officer that you can help them grow their business. When you can show them exactly step-by-step how you're going to grow their business, then they look at you and say, "When can we get started?" Your paycheck is the direct value that you bring to the marketplace. The more value you bring to your referral partners, the more you help them grow with your business, and the more money you'll ultimately make.

I can't remember who said it, but I've heard it on more than one occasion, "Price is only in question in the absence of value." This cannot be a more true statement. In the mortgage business we're typically all within one-eighth of a point of each other. Why should they use you over someone else? That's where value comes. Right now as I sit here and write this book, I'm adding new real estate agents and loan officers every day. I'm generating 70 to 90 leads a week to help others grow their business. I'm having the time of my life doing it.

Chapter 14

Revelations

I've learned a lot in my 40 years on this earth, but I've really learned a lot in the 15 years since college. The main thing that I learned is that I'm a fucking winner. I've often said that successful people will figure out ways to be successful. It's not because they are the brightest, fastest, or strongest. I will be successful because I know one thing about myself that others don't. I will outwork, outlearn, and out-implement everyone around me.

There was a time in my life that I limited myself, because I felt like maybe I didn't deserve it. There was a time in my life that friends and family made me feel bad for the success and the things that I had. You may have people that shame you for your nice homes, nice cars and your nice things. What I've found with those people is that they didn't see all the hard work that went in behind it. They only wanted to be around to judge the success.

There's a great meme I saw once on Facebook with a picture of an iceberg. It showed the top of the iceberg as a success, but what it didn't show is that underneath the water, it was five times the size. That was the hard work, the sleepless nights, the stress, the empty bank account, the fear, the anxiety, and the questions. They were not there when Hope and I didn't have any money to pay our mortgage or our other bills.

For those of you that are willing to put in the work, out-learn, and out-implement, I assure you that the journey is well worth it. What I learned through two career blows and the death of both of my parents was that I could still be OK. No one was going to come and save me. It was all up to me.

I made a decision in 2014, after my mother passed away, that I was going to bet on me, because two of my three biggest supporters were now gone. Hope and my children were all that was left to keep me heading in the right direction and I would not let them down. They are my *why*. I know my father often told people that he was very proud of me, but that was something that he never really told me. He was the type of father who if I got a 95, he asked me why it wasn't a 97. I can remember as a kid it used to really piss me off. I'd think, "It's still an A, what more do you want?" One of the lessons that my parents taught me was to never be satisfied with the status quo. Never be satisfied with average.

It took me a long time to realize that athleticism, attractive looks, and God-given talents will only get you so far. The people that are truly willing to put in the work through imperfect action are the ones that will be standing on top, the most successful.

Chapter 15

What's Next?

I have been asked a lot recently why I'm writing a book. I had to stop and think about what was the purpose behind this. If you've ever written a book, you know that it's very time-consuming and challenging. As you've read in many of these chapters, I'm a pretty busy person. Not only because I want to be, but because I have to be. I have a family and employees that rely on me.

I felt that it was important to write this book for a number of reasons. I wanted to share with people that it's OK to fail. It's OK to have doubts and not know what you're going to do. It is not OK to lay there and play the victim. I wanted to show that you, too, can be a success if you are willing to do what others aren't.

I have built teams and multi—million dollar businesses time and time again, even after setbacks have come into my life. This book was written because I am hoping that it will inspire and help people. I've been fortunate enough to have great mentors that believed in me and helped guide me to success. I wanted to take what I have learned and help other people become great.

I made a decision this year to give back.

2016 was going to be the year that I lived in abundance. I wanted to take people with me on my journey of success. That's the difference between successful people and people who do not have your best intentions. The successful people will share with you their secrets to success. I tell you this, as I tell my friends and family, because I love you, not because I mean to brag. I hope what I'm able to do is inspire you. If I can do it, anyone can do it. I'm more than willing, just as many have been before, to share with others what has made me successful. I have learned that it is important that I take my friends and family on the journey with me.

What you do with this information is totally up to you. Here's what I know, 95 percent of you will read this, be inspired, and won't do shit with it. I won't be there to babysit you. I wrote this book to help people who truly want to put in the work, who truly want to figure out where they want to go in life.

In four short years, I've built a business with millions in revenue, multiple employees, multiple locations, and very high earning potential. It didn't happen overnight. In 2011, when I sat in my 9-year old daughter's room and told her that we couldn't go to McDonald's because we didn't have the money, I couldn't imagine where my life would be today.

So, I want to encourage you to always look to do better. Never wish for others' failures, only wish them success. I wish all of my competitors, and even people that don't like me, success. I just want to be a little bit more successful than the guy sitting next to me. If nothing else, one thing I hope you take away from this book is that things will never be perfect. Don't wait. Do it today. Tomorrow may not be here. Go be great for yourself, for your family, and for your community.

If you are a Loan Originator or Real Estate Agent struggling to consistently grow your business and take it to the next level and want to learn more about the mentorship programs I offer, feel free to email me at chad@imperfectactiontakers.com to set up a time for a free consultation.

You only get one shot at this life so go all in and do BIG THINGS!

Be GREAT!